Bernadette Cremin

Miming Silence

First published in 2009
by Waterloo Press (Hove)
95 Wick hall
Furze Hill
Hove BN3 1PF

Printed in Palatino 11pt by
One Digital
54 Hollingdean Road
East Sussex BN2 4AA

Cover design and typesetting © Matilda Persson 2009
Cover photo © Julian Harvey 2009
Author photo © Mike Wheelan 2009

A CIP record for this book is available
from the British Library

ISBN 978-1-906742-14-0

By the same author

Sensual Assassin, audio CD (State Art, available at www.bernadettecremin.co.uk, 1999)
InsideSkin, film and pamphlet (Indifference Productions, 2001)
Home, DVD (The South, 2003)
Perfect Mess (Biscuit Publishing, 2006)
Mutual Territory, audio CD (State Art, 2007)
Speechless (Waterloo Press, 2007)

Acknowledgements

I am thankful to you (the reader) for simply picking me up! I sincerely hope you'll find something that deserves your time among these pages...

I (yet again) find myself blessed by the smart eye and seamless friendship of Jan Goodey who has been more supportive over my writing-years than he may realise.

I'd also like to thank Matilda Persson and Alan Morrison for their generosity, editorial advice and (especially Matilda) for her artistic input and patience!

I would of course like to thank Dr Simon Jenner for continuing to support my poetry as have Keiron Phelan and Arts Council England.

I'd also like to mention *The London Magazine* and *the Recusant* who have both published poems that appear in this collection.

Last but not least I'd like to thank those who (albeit unwittingly!) have inspired some of these poems...and as ever God and his mysterious ways!

Contents

for Jazz

As soon as I speak I am betrayed by the situation.
I am betrayed by the person listening to me simply
as a function of communication.
I am betrayed by my choice of words…
Jean Genet

Miming Silence

1

'One, two, buckle my shoe' (trad)

BRIGHT SATURDAY

Spring unwinds
as a hush of buttercups
curtsy in the tiny breeze

then the soft punch
of jasmine takes my mind
by the hand back to May 1973.

I was a ponytail and freckles
my dress a wash of bluebells
that bright Saturday.

That bright Saturday
Mr Jim didn't come home
from work

That bright Saturday that
peeled his wife's smile off
and she stopped…

baking miss-shapes
pushing red sweets
through the broken fence.

That bright Saturday
her garden began to grow
so slowly into lonely

a death-scape of dandelion heads
incestuous weeds and an apple tree
that surrendered into a buckled fist

a vice of thistles spread
like disease round the ankles
of her back-combed roses

and barbs and thorns clung
like lunatics to the legs
of her gloss-white beehive

that I dared myself to stand
too close to, pressed my head
against wood and drenched

myself in its malicious music —
that's where I learned the sound
of stings breeding

and how to decipher the bizarre
maps that trapped wings beat
when trying to escape the dark.

The fascination with threat
that still keeps me awake
when the night doesn't fit.

FLESH COLOURED RUBBERS

Stuffy buses, wet hair and stringy chat
remind me of school trips to places with roofs
souvenir pencils and flesh coloured rubbers.

The blue and white scarf mum got from the catalogue,
the itchy green mittens I lost twice on purpose,
plump spam sandwiches, pink wafers and *Quavers*.

The Tupperware cup with a bitten lip and dodgy lid
that leaked sticky squash into the toffee-plastic satchel
that dad got off the market the day Elvis died.

UNCLE TOM'S WAKE

I was too young to understand,
too young to escape Aunt Teresa's
back-combed laughter, her titian rinse
and creased cleavage.

I was too young to understand
the rebel songs that Uncle Eamon
was always too drunk to remember
and the truth about Uncle Owen

he was never drunk enough to forget.

POLAROID

I still dread August
remembering the white cotton
holidays at uncle Fred's.

How he watched my hips happen
and soft-prodded my nipples
with the pad of his thumb

they swell pinker and plumper
every summer he'd whisper
unbuttoning them clumsily.

I still dread August.
Still stick pins into the black
and white Polaroid

where aunty Pam forced me
to stand, poised like thunder
under a ridiculous tree.

TANGLED SOLDIERS

Liam screamed
till his head verged
on bursting

when I couldn't find
his red Matchbox bus
in Dad's buckled suitcase

so Mrs Devlin kidnapped
Action Man and a fist full
of tangled soldiers

from young Dermot's
big toy box next door
because...

Aunty Anne has no boys toys
as God has seen fit
not to bless her with a son but

I want to be like her when I grow up
because she has fat-flowered towels
that smell of Irish

and wears Avon lipstick
called dolly-mix-pink
and is pretty enough

to arrange the flowers in church.

DÉJÀ VU

She had an ink-stained
red pencil case with a sticky zip
that smelled of wood shavings

wore white knee-high socks
like the ones his bearded jokes
told her at bedtime.

Now, 31 years on
she signs for the release
of his personal effects

from Essex General Hospital:
£29.00 in used notes and three coins,
no cards, no copper change

one wallet, leather, black,
one Pulsar watch, black strap (working),
two Yale keys on a brass ring

one white cotton handkerchief, blue trim (soiled),
a Ladbrokes docket for the three thirty at Haydock
and the photo he took of her first day at school:

new blue bobbles and an awkward tie,
her small smile bitten and frozen in time
as it aimed dead straight into the lens

like a terrified surgeon.

2

'Spending long summer days indoors writing
frightening verse to a buck-toothed girl in
Luxembourg' (The Smiths)

SOFT FENCE

The party was a soft fence against the weather.

In the corner an army of Stella stood to attention
unopened, watching the war —

the slaughter of bottles and cans crushed
and abandoned like one night stands.

In the hall, small talk fought with stubborn music —
I tried to unlace a ginger conversation but when

he offered me a cigarette I wanted to
be the someone who wasn't scared of

smoking it
again.

Against the kitchen wall a brittle couple fucked
like spastic ballerinas, the plain girl grunting

politely as he threw himself into her
aimlessly.

I watched his bared teeth and thought
of a fish spine snapped by a rapid hand —

the mess a hook makes of a throat,
the secret that was melting in my mouth.

Yes the party was a soft fence but I knew
the weather will always wait.

A patient wolf.

GROWING PAINS

Silence was
the lullaby you left
to keep Susan awake.

She wasted her teenage
hunting for the reason
in your record collection

she untangled Joy Division,
Two-Tone and Ska until
anorexia finally broke her.

She unstitched each lyric
gnawed every chorus and verse
punished herself like a thin dog

because you left her the red thing
that any glass shape can cut
out of a wrist and...

I hope you had time to panic properly
time to regret the mess you left
for your mother to find

time to watch your soft pulse
throb like love-sex into the warm bath
you drew like a Hollywood cliché.

I hope you had time to panic properly.

See now I just remember you
as the one with fat fingers
that Susan even bothered to kiss

another would-be local hero
that hungry girls fell in love with
until their periods started.

But I never will forget your dad
in my dad's chair drinking whiskey
asking me to write your eulogy

because I wrote poetry
and wouldn't let him down.
So it was for him alone

that I took a filthy drug at your funeral
so that I was capable to stand at the altar
to tell lies for your mother

to a too young congregation
that stood in their older brothers' suits
smart shoes and awkward black ties

casting their aimless prayers into the sky
while I begged God for a selfish frost
to chew the football pitch you ran across

every fucking Sunday.

KING PIN
for Jan Goodey

He was god:

Oxblood 18 hole
steel toe-capped
Doc Martins

skin-fit bleach jeans,
khaki Harrington,
starched Ben Sherman.

He was suede-shaven
a flea-run running
temple to nape

an Indian ink
cut here tattoo
across his neck

a silver ring in his top lip,
a chipped front tooth,
he was a Cocky Fuck.

The handsome King
in a scrambled gang
of lads

who used to crash
round the garages
getting wasted

on *Thunderbird*
cider, spliff and glue.
He used to sniff until

he tasted blood
'till his shadow started
arguing back in backwards.

his broken head pressed
against an un-tuned radio
moaning two-tone into one note.

I kissed him once at Steve's 18th.
I was *out of my tree*
on Benylin and sherry.

He cracked my lipstick,
his relentless erection
pressed against my left thigh —

he tasted like a deep breath
in my father's shed
or the sixth form art room

where my lovesick compass
engraved his name in my desk.
I loved him in spite of good advice

because he dared me to let him stare into my eyes.

SCARLET MOHICAN

From the top deck back seat
a Scarlet Mohican with acne brags
to a Bleach Blonde nose ring
about becoming a dad in June.

He jokes about 'gettin' a fuckin' job
and 'avinta move autov his nan's'.
(She giggles at the thought of him
trapped in prams and nappies.)

'I wouldn't give a fuck' he shouts
teenage loud 'but I needed a fuckin'
chisel to get into her fuckin' knickers
for the fuckin' crap shag it was

in the shed at Dev's party.'
(She can't believe Dev's twenty)
'Is he still a fuckin' psycho'
(her blood demands?).

ALBINO

Anna consumed me

(not in the same way as Sister Martha's 'tash
each others' tits, snoggin' or *Top of The Pops*)

but that summer curiosity wore me like lovesickness
as I became slowly obsessed with the new girl Anna —

Sister Patricia always hid her in well-intended corners
to protect her soft eyes from sunlight like a thin plant.

She was exempt from outdoor sport without a note
which made Helen McKeever angrier than maths;

and I remember how mad I got the day that Eamon joked
that she caught it from a rabbit, and nicknamed her 'Lettuce'.

I never did believe her excuses when I invited her to drool
over the lads' football practice and swap make-up and gossip with us.

I once sat behind her in French and was transfixed by the opaque
Ponytail, pale and shy as an ivory bride tied by thin lemon ribbon

and surprised when I realised that the pop-star-dark glasses
she was allowed to wear in class were the jailer's, which locked her

rose-tinted vision in.

CARAMEL COCOA CLUB

Nan was livid as vinegar
whenever she smelled

the kaleidoscope of butterflies
dance around my perfume

or heard the sapphire Capri
that used to call for me

to go *run like a slut*.
To party with hot snow

in the seamless corridors
of the Caramel Cocoa Club

where muscular baselines
melted me into soft knots

and incisor smiles
convinced me to drink

cocktails that matched my eyes
and a cunning tongue

with a matador's hips
hid his dirty secret in me.

3

'Can someone open the windows and let the fish out?
…milk me' (Miranda)

FAÇADE

It's nearly time to meet my jitter of muesli-eating friends.
Time to pretend I care about the inconvenient weather

that's left a haphazard veil of frost across the washing
that I've forgotten to take in for the last three days!

Dr SANJEZ'S HANDS

I sit in the front row

of Dr Sanjez's lecture
every week to watch her

fingers
pale as patience —

how they hack mid-air
attacking language

bending and stretching
Spanish like lies. Miming.

Her nails are gently
varnished scarlet

each cuticle lured
into its bed

like ten livid
infants screaming

but the tiny garnet
on her ring finger's

flirted with marriage
too long now

(lost faith in the promise
her expectation made?).

It is nearly lunchtime
again and I haven't heard

a single word again
just doodled a chain

of daisies and swastikas
across the page again

and the re-take waits
impatiently in my diary

circled in red
like an angry bull.

mOthErS

Dead babies
are given
soft names

because
it's easier
to whisper.

CATHERINE

Catherine pushed the wick back
into the wet green wax

with the handle of John's toothbrush
when he phoned to apologise for another

traffic jam again. Then she threw

the teacup he stole from the Trent hotel
nineteen years ago against the garage wall

(the trophy he won for her virginity
before leaving her to count sheep).

FRILLY SOLDIERS

Tina is bored, she's lonely, so on weekday mornings she escapes via *Unwins* and, armed with a bottle of cheapest red, twenty *B&H, skins* and sweets for the kids, she goes round Debs... to get wasted in a *hint of a tint* prison on a floral print sofa in a living room cut from a catalogue picture and *stacked on the plastic...*

It's an exact replica from some glossy brochure, her lifestyle's designed by the junk-mail fliers that get punched through the letterbox by other numb housewives for their little bit of cash on the side, so they can by patches and call them luxuries, to buy or swap and pop their Valium and Temazepam with the lard-arse-tart at bingo.

But Tina and Debs prefer *grog and spliff* to toast the bailiffs with when they come (again) to reclaim the new kitchen sink, the three piece suit, last month's fads and must haves, the designer labels for the kids, because *Reebok, Boss, Lacoste* cost more from the catalogue but she didn't think.

And now the new washing machine can't get her *Calvin Kline* T-shirt clean, the latest advert can't get the claret out, and the hock's pocked her white cotton, like blood stained medals won in the battle she's lost with herself.

And all too soon morning yawns into afternoon, the kids are beaten into submission by head-butting cartoons and *Play Station* because mum's given in to every tantrum — every whim, just to keep the sound of fun down.

By now she knows her new bloke will be *giving it large* up the pub; looking for work in the bottom of a pint pot, or chatting up the blonde who signs him on when he bothers to show up, or investing his dole cheque in Ladbrokes

where *Good Luck's* a *dead cert*
on the three thirty favourite at Haydock
again!

But Tina's stuck, relying on *Jerry Springer* to convince her she's got her life in order compared to the antics of the sad exhibitionists who hang their dirty washing out in public for raucous applause.

Tina and Debs, *the petticoat comrades; frilly soldiers* doing women's work, fighting their war behind a locked front door, dulling the pain with raw alcohol and repeated soap operas, but their heroines still don't live happy ever after the second, third, fourth, time around.

ONCE UPON AN AUTUMN

It began once upon an autumn.

She's kept the crisp linen napkin
from their first date
in a crimson restaurant.

A silver coffee-shop spoon
from a fairy tale weekend
in a hotel with a French accent

twenty-nine beer mats
from twenty-nine Sunday lunches
in a cosy rose-rimmed pub

and a vanity bag of corks
pulled on special occasions
that she's forgotten. Now

she lends him skin to pay
for the apologetic bouquets
he buys from the corner shop

bunches of colour tamed
and suffocated in cellophane
double knotted at the neck

with gaudy nylon bows
that she rips with her teeth
over the kitchen sink.

He has taught her
how to hate properly
how to bleed on demand

how to watch mascara run
in a locked bathroom
how to hunt slowly

how to master patience exactly
like an anorexic kneeling
at a midnight fridge.

SOLEMN

I am here to book fun, in eight months away.

Across the manic carpet
behind a restless desk
a plump 20-something
agitates PC keys.

I flick through magazines
of pristine everywhere's
I've never been
never met in an atlas
or at party chit-chat.

On page six —

A vanilla beach — a flesh circus
of six packs and unwrapped breasts
tassels of lean bikinis stretched and
tenderised by salt water simmer
under a pantomime sky.

On page nine —

a love-drunk couple sip chilled fizz
and beam at their symmetrical children
watching them chase melting ice cream
through fumbling fingers, past wrists
across palms and down arms

with giggling tongues.
In the distance a toned teenager
throws a rainbow beach ball
across a staple onto the next page
where his girlfriend waits on tiptoe.

Impossible colours spill through the brochure
into European cities where sophists graze
on newspapers at pavement cafés

and greedy tourists with spiteful cameras
bite lumps out of the architecture.

I continue browsing a world away
until a raincoat with a wet wife
coughs and I stop at page twenty eight
where a solemn mountain suffocates
under a mistake the snow has made.

THE REASON FOR THURSDAYS

I paint my nails an uncomfortable colour
and wear complicated underwear on Thursdays.

I work at an office in a nest of cheap body sprays,
oily humour, ill-fitting bras and smokers' coughs.

I was parked here by a break-down four years ago
at the furthest desk from the window, but still can't

risk the view. Every morning I watch Fat-John
digress by the coffee machine peeling gossip

and making up drunken fights out with the lads
and one-night-stands with girls he'll never smell.

Pat (the senior clerk) digs her words
out of the stubborn Manchester accent

and in spite of the weather
is always unbuttoned

two buttons too much
so her crinkled cleavage can breathe

as it suffocates the gold plate gate chain
that spits back the fluorescent light.

But on Thursdays Mr Elvyane's black attaché
walks past my desk at the same steady, steady pace

leaving a graze of insistent aftershave
on his way to the deli on St. James Street

where he orders bespoke sandwiches,
sips black bitterness, smokes Turkish cigarettes

and flirts with the sallow waitress
with a chestnut ponytail and soft hips.

I hang my week on Thursdays, they solve
the ache that I nurse like a sin.

MOTHERS' MEETING

The clouds are grumbling
unable to commit to weather —
how dull... how very, very dull —

paper plates and sunflower napkins,
scattered plastic forks and spoons —
the picnic had tried to be fun

(but I just want to dance on the grass
throw stones at smitten young couples
lick the ice cream man... scream).

See, I've been tetchy all afternoon —
snapped the kids into real tears
and quivering lower lips

threatened them with early beds
and stopped pocket money until...
forever and ever... Amen.

And I know I've stalked arguments
with the other mousy-curl-mums
in their pastel coloured T-shirts...

(just long enough...
to hide the stretch marks...)
thick thigh jeans and Adidas trainers

their lipstickless laughter,
support bras, practical sandals
and easy-to-keep ponytails —

'See, I've tried the small talk-babble
about post-natal depression,
raw nipples and sleepless nights

(but I need to contemplate pearls.
The profanity that beauty is simply
a consequence of irritation…)

and I can't stop imagining men
with massive hands and cockney accents
who grab your arse and call you 'doll'…

I want to paint the bedroom stupid orange
and have deranged sex with a stranger
who drinks Guinness with gin chasers –

(I am raw for nonsense and futile fun:
I want to forget the kids' names
wear vermilion leather and fishnets to bed.)

My husband suggests I drink more water,
take the stairs instead of the escalator,
have a lavender bath or St John's Wort

stop listening to Bjork and Amy Winehouse —
and I do love him (in a water-colour way)
but I envy the way he loves me.

The weekend is tomorrow:

so I'll kick-start into *wife-gear* again;
strip beds, wash football kits,
work shirts and pick up the pinstripe

from the girl with bitten nails,
chav-chains and a pink mobile phone
with a Beyonce ring tone

at the launderette on my way to Asda.
I am so jealous of her hungry cleavage —
her licence for mind-bending indifference.

BLIND LION

Jean groomed my wedding
into a militia of plan B's
that anticipated creases, sticky-
fingers, raised eyebrows, tears.

She preyed on the only promise
I'll ever make like a blind lion
in an abattoir, honed me into
whale bones, an impossible waist.

— an ivory silk coffin of shallow breaths —

My bespoke sister chose my bouquet,
a calligraphy of swollen yellows
and as usual was followed everywhere
by glances and her chorus of malt curls.

My hapless locks were bribed by a tiara
and a pinch of silver glitter by a timid
Susan — someone with naked fingers
that Jean had sniffed off the internet.

Jean ushered me like a clumsy puppy
into tamed poses with the same strangers
I only ever meet in photos, who sometimes
share a surname, a hint of jaw line.

My smile fevered on poised lipstick
like a numb trapeze artiste anticipating
the flash, the smack in the back of my eye
as the paid stranger with ideal teeth

bit another moment out of me…

Confetti is a pretty bomb,
a chaotic tissue of hearts
blown across tarmac,
whispered into corners

airless places.

SHORTCUTS

I write shorthand
in green crayon
on the unopened bills.
I lean against the kettle

paint transparent swastikas
across your shaving mirror
with clear nail varnish.
Words. Pictures. Shortcuts.

I scribble any-colour biros
on the back of my left hand
because I like the medical smell
of coal tar and rough towels

and I scratch a slow death-wish
across your back when you lie
heavy on me whispering
deep into my hair

telling me over and over
how in love you are
with my stillborn sister,
my traitor, my breathless twin

because you know I am listening.

SARAH'S HUSBAND

takes showers to confirm his masculinity.

He's pruned his time to exactly seven minutes
having read an article in a Sunday supplement
that concluded this to be the national average
for a moderately active man of his age.

He insists on *Detol*, *Palmolive* and *Vosene*
peppermint emulsion and apple-white tiles
(she once joked that the walls matched the soap
forgetting how threatening he still finds affection).

Every weekday he moles his lunch breaks away
in a back street café where a flexible teenager
with a pencil behind his ear clatters bangles
and mumbles stormy songs.

He always orders *Mothers' Pride,* white
bursting with any red meat and mayonnaise
and trespasses the tabloid for tits
at the table next to the fire exit

where he carved his initials on April 5th '76
with the fidgeting penknife the forensics
found among the debris that the fire left
in his older brother's flat.

GRAHAM'S WIFE

Over the years she's learned to ignore him
sniffing through the rubbish on Wednesdays

checking for her little mistakes, desperate
for clues to how she spends her days.

Now she always leaves an un-rinsed tin
or two and a few unsorted magazines

to justify his complaints
and never mentions the hours he wastes

tinkering in the shed after work.
The endless trimming and preening

loose ends off the garden.

BACKWARDS

As expected
the train will be late —

I won't buy a ticket
and take a seat facing
backwards. I'll watch

a few crumpled students
dribble off at Falmer
then browse the D.O.Y.

brochure, circle reviews,
scribble across photos,
recite my 9 times table

backwards. Then I'll text
the friend I only ever text
on trains to tell him

I'm on a train. He does the same
(and neither of us wonder why).

4

'A mother's son has left me sheer' (Portishead)

LOVE

smudge me.

THIS ROOM

If I sit at that angle
it's nearly comfortable

but I fail when
you decipher my smile

the crack it makes
across my face.

I am a tower of ash
in a sorry wind

when you hold me,
when we pretend

to be just friends
as we kiss cheeks

and I leave this room.
These corners, these stains

this wallpaper cage
that watched us

two cowards scared
of love out loud.

Where you shuffled me like music,
steered my strings with clever wrists

nursed me with white noise
and the thud of your pulse

and I utterly miss this room
when I am everywhere else

snared in some handsome gaze,
held too close by another shirt

a pattern that I don't understand.

PATIENCE

An unread bible
another hotel room
trivial as logic.

Here is that moment
again when silence bites
behind my teeth… baiting

patience.

I wait for you slowly
to press your fingerprints
into me like benign thorns

as I count the backs
of your teeth
with my tongue.

You spell French
prayers incorrectly
through my hair

then across my forehead
then bless my eyelids
backwards.

We watch our stare
fight in mid-air
as we stand face to face

like brave things.

SMALL BED

Take me to your small bed
let's smudge into us again
under the dust and cobwebs

that cling to the ceiling
above our heads
craving safety.

Take me to your small bed
where shadows fail into corners
harmless as deaf whispers.

Take me to your small bed
let's pray into each others' mouths
kiss like clouds and gentle blades.

Let your ink pen bleed
into the pine bedside cabinet
like a broken soldier

and let the dozing roses
crane their long necks
around the scorched lampshade

to watch our muscular tongues
eager teeth and curious fingers
lick and scratch skin-maps

as we feed on each other
like blind vampires
hunting touch.

Take me to your small bed
let our pillow-talk and belly laughs
trip each other up as our words chase

our words with their eyes closed.

Take me to your small bed
let me wear your sweat and spit
like a silent perfume —

behind my ears
across my breasts
between my legs.

Take me to your small bed
and let's surrender like smoke rings
in half-dark.

OUT OF BOUNDS

I lie half open, abandon
my supple imagination
to this gentle danger.

We concoct time
in warm coffee shops
mauling *shoulds* and *oughts*

skirt the weird silence
that shy half casts
across conscience.

We translate blushes
unfinished sentences.
Bite the bit.

We are licking a loaded gun
rolling a polished bullet
around our tongues

but I forgive this crime
because it takes me
to the dark side

to watch white roses grow.

SOMETIMES

Sometimes I think
I love you enough but

sometimes I don't
understand green.

Sometimes I choose
words I can't spell

to challenge my accent
and sometimes I can forget it

and I cherish that moment…
just before the world catches

me up.

DIZZY

I wore wasp-scent,
a dizzy dress, no shoes —

you wore a broken promise
and an uncertain attitude.

You drove too fast
for me to notice...

took me to burgundy places
where leather strangers

licked each others' wounds
like clever knives. But

I needed that white lie
you gift wrapped in a kiss

to teach me to yield
with my eyes half-shut

and how to bite my tongue
just gently enough to stop

it wasting words on love.

THE LITTLE THINGS

It's because you

whistle and polish your brogues midweek,
pinch my arse that bit too hard in Sainsbury's
always at the busiest checkout just loud enough
for the earwigs and cashiers to hear.

It's because you

pretend to forget my birthday every year,
can punctuate my ripe temper with a grin
and have been on chapter ten of the Ovid
since nine bikes and two girlfriends ago.

It's because you

keep a world of sketches and notebooks
in an unlocked red box under the bed,
hand back my mistakes unwrapped —
it's the little things make loving you easy

scary and jealous of myself.

SCRIBBLING IN THE MARGIN

Lying in bed I listen
to the door click at your heel

the eleven steps it takes
to the elevator and then

that pause as you walk
across the car park.

Next, your ignition kicks in
and takes you scurrying

back to another bed
where someone is waiting.

I stretch my leg
into the wet patch you left

and reinvent the women
who have wound around you.

The ones who live in sage places —
Sloane Square, Hampstead Heath —

who wear autumnal silk
and flirt with their exact manicures.

Those with confused perfume
that you bring back in your hair

for me to play with
and that one whose name

you pretend to forget
when our pillow talk falls

off
the kerb.

Today is Monday —
you'll be back at ten

so I'll waste the morning
finding things to avoid

and in the afternoon I'll hide
behind a mud-moss face pack

bite my nails
and shave your territory

choose moody music
to moan like a porcelain whore

and dress Mandy the mannequin
in your favourite bra

the one you spent your dole on
that abandoned afternoon in Camden

and just before the door clicks and
you find me waiting where I was left

I'll light two slim damson candles
to whisper a rumour around the room.

PHYSICS

He is desperate as a young car crash—

obsessed with its curves, angels, straight lines
his ripe mind calculates the arch of its spine

the cusp of its neck, it is the immaculate
slut. His tongue is raw from licking the scars

its demands inflict on him, its cracked kisses
and broken petals... its uneasy things.

But he still believes that one day he will un-
suck the handle of the fat room open and

bloom like a peacock among the grinning prisms
that chisel seamless white into obedient rainbows.

But a life wasted on waiting has broken him
into a clever mess of questions breeding

pirouetting across his intellect like a ballerina
hunting inertia with vinegar in her eyes.

Its lies have pushed him toward measured steps
cautious as a bald nerve hovering above a wasp

and each night it squats in his sleep
swells like loss... each pulse

more eager than the last to spill and scurry
like impatient mercury into the fractures it crafts.

It haunts his blood... has driven him into whiskey
bolted him in a cage of greedy details

but he knows the keyhole is on the inside
and the door unlocked.

TWOSOME

You mouth slowly
at me across company

then lick your lips
to seal our unfinished.

You know how to
pace me like a diet

where to hold me
when my dream fidgets.

You are sexier
than an angled mirror

when you dance with me
like an unseen disease

double knotting my strings
like a spiteful child

when you prowl around me
like the underwear

you misspell in texts
and I cherish this risk

our mistake is taking.

MAGIC

He blushes like egg shell
as her knees bend and
then bend again.

He whispers tender filth
to the nape of her neck —
he needs to think things.

She cuts a new wound in him
swells his fist into a punch
that can't quite reach

she has convinced him
he can smell a buttercup
glazed in blood

or conjure a cough
to purr in his throat
like a smart cat.

She lets his spell meander
through her hair, lets him
plant tricks behind her ears.

Together they amuse the plain time —
she, a mess of sequins and feathers,
he, a bored magician

shuffling her pulse in the back row.

PIROUETTE

We concoct supple danger
in a Chelsea wine-bar

where wounded jazz
fractures the baby grand.

We play intricate games
like preened rats

leave scenarios poised
eager to dive like blades

from the tips of our tongues
as we play with breath but

I stop
when you dare me

to pirouette closer to the edge
where indelicate waits patiently.

And instead I imagine tracing
neat gin around your lips

with a Japanese paintbrush
or the subtle flavour of a blush.

SLITHER

Kiss me like anaesthesia —
let's foster the moment
slow dancing makes

take me somewhere stupid,
pretend it makes a difference
for as long as it takes.

Please call me Madeleine,
it will make things easier
when we bend the curve

when we juggle blades
and hunt for the soft place
our fingers can still smell

when we gloss over the mess
that life makes hushing scars
begging each other

for one more sliver of fear.

THE RIM

Today has been waiting
since we started pulling
wings off things

hunting ugliness
like dirty kids.
We wanted this.

To covet each other
like cheap souvenirs
cracking patiently.

But now I run
my finger round the rim
In some attempt to find

where things end. And begin.

5

'You can not kickstart a dead horse… you just cross yourself and walk away' (Thom Yorke)

POSTCARD

Posting jealousy home, sealed with a kiss.

NERVOUS

My fingernails are bitten
into surrender

and my pen flickers
across paper

like nervous mascara.
Mistakes follow me

everywhere
like a child's ghost

when I am too dangerous.
I frighten myself

into corners on purpose
to face the fact

that I do still exist
when the light shuts.

I stuff nonsense
into a bottom drawer

like a dusty spinster —
a kleptomaniac.

ROSEWOOD

I've put a deposit on the rosewood bureau
that's been sulking under months of dust
in the antique shop window.

It will take me nineteen Mondays to buy it
out of misery and welcome it to the scrabble
of other impractical furniture I've bought slowly

to introduce it to the colours, smells and sounds
my life makes before I stand it against the wall
like a soldier, praying for bullets.

THE GREASY MAN

I work as night receptionist
at *The Bella Vista* bed and breakfast —

it's easy money, The Greasy Man
never mentions the buxom doodles

I leave behind like clues,
the everythings I forget to do.

He knows I buy fags
from the petty cash

help myself to the messy
ice cream that licks me back

and turns a blind eye to the curious
optics (the mistakes whiskey makes).

The Greasy Man has lent me to Alison
and she draws me like a poultice.

She has invited me to waltz
in her soft-storm

taught me how to chew colour
from a schooner like a patient cat

how to trace a lip... an armpit...
an incisor in the dark

and now my nightmare is addicted
to the taste of her sling-backs

and the curves she makes
in that black satin hip-hug skirt

that clings like penance
between her legs.

Me and Alison like to play games.
We make The Greasy Man beg

then we get just drunk enough
to hurt for him like warm snow

and I let him rest his head
against my inner thigh

close enough for him
to smell me

while Alison winds
his stray nape hairs tight

anti-clockwise and we listen
to him cry like a pale child

mauling damage.

WHY

No one knows why
he hates Mozart so much

he tried to explain it once
to a shaving mirror

in a Premier Lodge
with a view of suburbia

but failed like a grey baby.

ANON

He's a saturated rain cloud
massaging the flood.

He stalks shadows round corners,
carves his odour into the dark.

His eyes are keen as sex
and I imagine him growing erect

winding his tongue around itself
when he jerks-off in public toilets.

His slit-lips stretch across his face
slash-thin as the greasy ponytails

I watch scoring heroin in the dead-
electric high street as rush hour begins.

Yet I feel a sad for this man
-locked into his counterfeit grin

I see he is terrified as bone china,
how he fails to forge the airbrushed smiles

and sun-kissed lifestyles that sneer
at him from between the tacky ads

for discreet sex, *Virgin* internet,
Sky, iPods and Wiis

hush-safe abortions and The Samaritans
that wink at him on the Brixton tube.

He is a black-booted toothache,
grey plasticine pushed down the crack.

Yet I feel a sad for this man.

ACHE

The clinic-sweet nurse said that *focus*
would lend me perspective but knew
that I could quote that textbook too.

Apologising for the *sharp scratch*,
she released the black elastic tourniquet
and bled another needle of me out.

I said I liked her brave new haircut,
a bleached crop that gifted her
ballerina cheekbones

in some attempt to put her at ease,
to let her know that it had stopped
hurting me long before she was born.

I watched her sift her pretty head
for a compliment to hand me back
but one day she'll understand

sometimes it's just kinder to smile.

JAYWALKING

My blade jaywalks across canvas,
bullies red to bleed to the edge

then it drags blue back
into a whirlpool of purples

and I wade through the mistakes
that colour makes.

Sometimes I sketch the high street
through my studio window

where the real world tick-
tocks in short skirts and T-shirts.

I stopped painting yellow
on the day that undid Jack

in a simple accident
that a child could manage —

the day his mother started to clip
the ends off sentences

bevelling her Dublin accent
as if apologising for the space it takes.

I paint purple for her,
force red into blue

like blood and bruises.

CARNEY

Folklore said the track had rusted over
(a feral testament to the unleashed boy)
so the grumble smothered by years of trees
intrigued me like hands in the dark.
Carney is a flint-built nest of half-truths
where frowning men murmur and women

simmer over nettle wine, haunting the muddy boys
with tight spun yarns of The Stokeens in the dark
scar of woodland, that tears like green chiffon over
Devlin Mountain. The town is possessed by Larn trees
that spill onto an incessant beach. Carney women
are lean, caramel-skinned and stubborn as truth.

I was enticed to visit it by a seamless woman
who wrote in violet ink. She wore her boy-
figure easily and was contradictory as an oak tree
on the cusp of summer. I was seduced by her dark
toffee skin and she by my name as we conjured vanity over
saki at a mutual friend's attempt at a party. She wore truth

and deceit in equal measure and flirted her arrogance over
awkward art, as we stung wit, snaring our shameless dark
humour by unstitching the polite room of other women.
She was born in Carney under a swollen Larn tree,
her twin brother torn from her by a calloused hand (a boy
that she still begs to unlock her prayers when the truth

confesses.) Then she unveiled the curse that shelters women
who ripen life in the dim season that beckons the Larn trees
to blossom crimson like blushing blood or wounded truth,
so as no other mother need ever have her warm boy
peeled from her, leaving his menacing silence to take over
her dark.

6

'I panic at the quiet times' (Turin Breaks)

NOVEMBER

November is nursing my weathered eye
so staring through the shallow horizon
I will this spiteful winter to subside.

The relentless grey has rendered me blind
and I crave the memory of cloud-cotton.
November is nursing my weathered eye

and no matter how hard the view may try
it can not comfort a storm with reason.
I will this spiteful winter to subside

so as the carnage can not be denied:
the damage abandoned by late autumn.
November is nursing my weathered eye

and the sun half-hides like a guilty spy
as frozen bullets bludgeon the season.
I will this spiteful winter to subside

and lend the aching sky to kinder light:
let weather undress like a chameleon.
November is nursing my weathered eye.
I will this spiteful winter to subside.

THE LITTLE VILLAGE

is an edge
a perforate
a frill

a lick
a something
small

a pattern tamed
to fit the landscape
green

a blind beauty
a bound bride waiting
for the inevitable

winter.
It shivers in thin wool
when the spiteful season

bites like an accident
waiting for strangers
to happen.

It is the promise
a Monday morning
breaks every week

the one step
escape with its eyes
shut.

It is polite as a
geologist's wrists
an excuse

for tourists, litter
photos and cream teas.
It doesn't understand

the underground,
the internet, patois
or mascara

but it yearns to grind
the neck of a base
across the bible

when it imagines
the smell of a pulse
breathing.

SNAPSHOT

Under the church porch
pastel cottons in ridiculous hats
huddle like orphaned puppies.

Over a daddy's shoulder
his little bundle of silk and taffeta
grizzles dribbling milk.

Just out of focus a blushing auburn
and nearly handsome best man
snatch a fag between smiles

make uncertain conversation
over Mary Benn's gravestone:
loving wife and mother

of Thomas Grace and Jessica 1916-

MEN AT WORK

This time next week
my mornings won't be
ripped open.

Banging Hammers
won't head-butt me
out of too-early sleep.

Elgar and Eminem
won't need to compete
for my attention.

I'll be able to hear
the chain of trains
filtering a world

of iPods, Navy Suits
and Weekday Perfume
to London again.

I'll welcome back
the familiar limp-pad
of the upstairs flat

but will miss the whistling
loop of 'Blue Suede Shoes'
and cockney banter

because this time next week
they'll be biting lumps out
of someone else's dreams

drinking tea from other mugs —
things will be back to normal
at Blondyn Court:

the lavender rinses
and walking sticks will crib
about dust in the lift.

The nip in the air.

ONCE A MONTH

Sunday morning turns in its sleep.
I rush across Preston Park
stunned by bright grass.

A milk float bimbles in the distance
and the smell of hangovers
frying breakfast amuses the air.

A flab of jogger in a spam crop top
plugged into an iPod
wobbles up the cycle path

and a pasty teenager pushing
a pram full of baby are happening
but the weather is missing.

Our monthly meetings are gnawing
my patience now like a spiteful doll.
Every time it's exactly the same…

I can predict that you'll be exactly
early, wearing a blue Ben Sherman
or a blue something else…

have some virus, splutter or cough —
and expect me to *tut* in the right place.
But I'm no longer interested in the gossip

you foster like a frustrated spinster
because the trivia you pamper
and pluck at through unwashed nets

is actually hurting me now.

SILVER

It flirts through
plate glass windows
cunning as sex

is simple as water yet
can buy time, a lover,
a conscience or murder.

It can bribe chic,
the exquisite and elegant
when held in a too-hot hand

it is louder than perfume
yet makes more silence
than candle-flame.

LACE

A tapered roll neck tames

her petite breasts that perch
like annoying apples —
her waist tapers effortlessly
into hips that just are.

Her ponytail beckons honey
and ginger slices into stripes
that give me thoughts to unwrap
when my day-dreams ripen.

She contrives a complexion
that is softer than the shadow
a wolf's tooth makes on snow
and I am feebled by her.

A woman... more intricate
than the lace handkerchief
that swarms in my damp palm.

WOMAN ON A TRAIN

I am amused that you
wear sunglasses on the tube —

how can that ugly pattern
suit you?

Your pale fingernails
humble me like soft hips

and the whisper-thin chain
that weeps from your wrist

stills me.
(How you

tame your crazy
raven hair

into fashion
with gold rope?)

At your feet
a bag of cashmere

nursed in pastel tissue
sits obediently —

you text someone
handsome and I listen

to a cello backstroke
through my headphones

and recline for a better view
of your jaw line.

MIMING SILENCE

PRETTY CAKE

I am still thrilled when I think
of the giggling ice-cream van

that used to swing its big hips
down our street.

(I am learning how to be
grateful for the lost things…

the days that wishbones don't
understand.)

But now and again I still chase
the place where a corner

ends and a wall begins
like a grazed knee kid

flip a coin, roll a dice
or bake a pretty cake

just for the sake of it.
Because now I can see

when a pale man doesn't trust
colour, when it's time to stop

defining improvised jazz,
time to step on the cracks

snap the spine of a book.